Delights
of Old

A little guide to delightful tearooms of
Perthshire, Angus and Dundee

by

Lorna McInnes

Teacups Press

www.teacupspress.com

First published in the UK in 2012 by Teacups Press
11 Lochy Terrace, Blairgowrie, Perthshire, PH10 6HY
www.teacupspress.com

A catalogue record for this book is available from the British Library

ISBN 978-0-9572930-0-7

Printed in Scotland by Danscot
www.danscot.co.uk

If, as an owner or member of staff in one of the tearooms in this book, you should notice any inaccuracy in any of the information contained herein, please inform the publisher (teacups@sent.com) and we will do our best to make appropriate changes for any future editions.

Especially for Bennet and Elizabeth McInnes
my two most delightful assistants

Acknowledgements

A big thank you to all my fellow bloggers and blog followers, for their friendship, encouragement, helpful advice and inspiring comments, to Godfrey Fitton for being a champion and drawing the map for me, to Kath at Danscot for her patient assistance and advice, to Flora for keenly advertising the book wherever she goes, and to the rest of my family and friends for all their supportive backing.

Special thanks to all my delightful assistants, especially delightful assistant no.1 for her lovely company, enviable capacity for tea and tearooms, and her useful comments, and delightful assistant no.2 for his constant enthusiasm, positivity and inspiring ideas.

Extra special thanks to all the tearooms in this book, for giving me something to write about and for serving up delicious treats while I go about it.

Contents

Introduction

Welcome to this little guide to delightful tearooms in the Perthshire, Dundee and Angus areas of Scotland. I hope you will find in these pages some tearooms to delight you. If you're a local, a visitor or an armchair traveller, I trust that this guidebook will give you some pleasant reading material for the odd moment when you fancy popping off to a tearoom, either in person or in your imagination.

What this book is

This is the first in what I hope will be a series of *Tearoom Delights*, gradually trotting out across different areas of the country. I've been enjoying tearooms (as well as cafés and coffee houses, please see **What exactly is a tearoom?** on page 14 for more on this point) for many years. In writing this book I thought it would be nice to recognise some of the wonderful tearooms that have served me tasty delights, as well as giving some recommendations to anyone looking for a lovely tearoom.

What this book isn't

I'm not a professional food and drinks critic and I'm not suggesting that the only tearooms worth visiting are those mentioned in this book. If someone else were writing this book, they would doubtless choose a different selection from mine and, therefore, I'm not claiming that this book is the last word on the matter. I deliberately haven't used phrases such as 'the best tearooms' because what suits one person's taste may not suit another. I'm not even sure I could explain exactly what it is that draws me to one tearoom over another, although there are certain standards that are met by all of the tearooms in this book.

Just because a tearoom is not featured in this book, does not necessarily mean it's not a fine establishment. I didn't want to include every tearoom in the area because a) they're not all to my taste, and b) the Yellow Pages or phone book already does that job. I may also have missed some real corkers, just by dint of not having discovered them yet.

Bonnie Scotland: Perthshire, Angus and Dundee

I feel very fortunate to live in Scotland, surrounded by beautiful and varied countryside, and I hope this little book might encourage people who maybe wouldn't otherwise have thought of visiting this area to come and see what it's like, as well as reminding those who know it well just how full of delights it is.

I've asked quite a few non-Scots what they know about Scotland or what comes to mind when they think of it, and the top answer has been – perhaps surprisingly for Scots themselves – Nessie, the Loch Ness Monster. In addition to Nessie, people often know about the mountains and glens, and perhaps typically Glencoe, from seeing striking photographs and paintings of such scenery.

Certainly, there are some parts of Scotland that attract considerably more tourists than others, particularly the cities of Edinburgh and Glasgow, and the spectacular western highlands. While I'm passionate about Scotland as a whole and very glad to sing the praises of the well known parts, there are many less well known areas that also have much to recommend them.

The region of Angus is a case in point. The area in general is pretty flat, although there are some rolling hills and glens, as well as an interesting coastline, but part of its charm lies in the lack of tourist attractions and the relative peace of the countryside (not that any of Scotland's countryside is particularly over-run with people).

Perthshire is more well known as a tourist destination, because of its wonderful mixture of hills, mountains, lochs and glens. It is often dubbed 'big tree country' due to the prevalence of interesting trees, many of them outstanding specimens. The county is not only home to the world's highest hedge (the Meikleour beech hedge, planted in 1745), but contains Europe's oldest tree (the Fortingall yew) and has become a haven for the world's most threatened conifer species through the iCONic rescue project. It is famed for its good walking, hiking and cycling country, with plenty of way-marked hill and forest trails, and is a great place for striking photo opportunities.

Dundee has an interesting history and is a popular city with students (I've heard several people who studied in Dundee rave about the place), and although it doesn't occupy much space in this book, it is worth a visit for the tearooms that are mentioned, and for the magnificent Discovery Point attraction, featuring the very boat that took Captain Scott to the Antarctic.

Walks

When I first had the idea of writing this book, I intended to include information about walks near to the tearooms featured, but then I realised that I would be repeating information that was already available in a more appropriate format elsewhere.

If walks are of interest to you, Perthshire is particularly well covered, and I can recommend an excellent series of books by Felicity Martin (details on her website: *www.catkinpress.com*). She currently has four volumes, each containing 12 walks around Perthshire, and her books are attractively produced in full colour. Another publisher, Pocket Mountains (*www.pocketmountains.com*), produces a range of colourful little guidebooks covering walking and cycling routes all over Scotland.

History and other information

In addition to walks, I thought about including some local history or other information for every location, as I sometimes do on my blog (see **Website updates** on page 20), but again I think this is already well covered by other books and it could easily have become another whole book in itself. If you pop into any good bookshop or tourist information centre in the areas covered in this book you will find a wealth of local tomes covering diverse topics about the areas concerned. Again, Perthshire is particularly well off for such writing, and the nicely laid out tourist information centre in Arbroath stocks a good range of titles covering Angus.

I asked my father (who is a great reader of such books) about local history, and he mentioned a few of his favourite topics: military roads, Queen Victoria, and wind farms. This may not, of course, be the sort of selection that would stimulate everyone, but I thought it might be of interest to include what he gave me by way of the few paragraphs on page 13.

He and I both like a nice wind farm (contentious, I know), and love to see trains on days out. Whenever I see a train as I'm driving around visiting tearooms, I repeat a little mantra of his: "It's always a good day when you see a train", and it makes me feel that all is right with the world and my day has suddenly improved immeasurably. I recommend it.

For general tourist information, such as places to visit, events being held, and accommodation options and bookings, please see Scotland's national tourist body, VisitScotland (*www.visitscotland.com*). They produce a paper brochure that covers the areas in this book, and they also have two extra websites available: *www.perthshire.co.uk* and *www.angusanddundee.co.uk.*

Leading on from Scotland's Year of Homecoming in 2009 (a calendar of events celebrating all things Scottish), 2012 was designated the Year of Creative Scotland. I thought it fitting to mention this in my book because the aim is *"to build on the momentum generated in 2009 and journey towards the next year of Homecoming in 2014 by promoting and celebrating Scotland as a culturally vibrant and creative nation to the people of Scotland and our visitors"*. I would like to support the project because this book exists to promote and celebrate all aspects of Scotland, most importantly its many delightful tearooms.

www.creativescotland.com

A bit of local history by Bennet McInnes

Military roads that were designed and built by General Wade and his successors from 1725 onward have been gradually upgraded to become some of today's main motor roads, including the A9 (also known as the Great North Road) and it is interesting to see how many routes have been developed in that way. Some stretches of the military roads have disappeared without trace and others are now barely discernible tracks across rough hillsides, but some have become minor roads and it is not too difficult to imagine the work involved in making them.

Queen Victoria's enthusiasm for holidays in Scotland was recorded in her diaries, which make interesting reading. Her journeys to and from Balmoral Castle (which is not far north of Perthshire) by train, by coach, and on her pony, and her visits to various large houses scattered around the country have led to the appearance of 'Victorian trails' which offer interesting walks and drives in areas that still have a Victorian flavour.

The development of hydroelectric power involved major engineering work in Perthshire that was regarded by many people as vandalism at the time but has now blended into the landscape and adds interest to it. The current construction of wind farms provokes similar reactions but some of us enjoy the sight of the magnificent new windmills which enliven some parts of the landscape.

What exactly is a tearoom?

According to the dictionary, it's an establishment where tea and light refreshments are served. This could also describe a café or coffee house, and much of the time all three terms are interchangeable.

Personally, although I am very happy to enter establishments calling themselves cafés or coffee houses, I like the word tearoom because of the connotations it presents to my mind. A tearoom suggests old-fashioned daintiness, the clink of fine china teacup on saucer, tasty beverages, delicious fluffy freshly baked scones and mouth-wateringly wonderful cakes and other small treats. A good tearoom can take your mind off your troubles, and make you feel you're being looked after and pampered for as long as it has your company.

Once you're settled in a good tearoom, and have perused the menu and made your choice, you begin to feel relaxed and transported to a better place. When the food and drinks are served, they should look appetising and, very importantly, live up to or exceed expectations on tasting. The ambience and service in the tearoom are also very important factors, and have a strong bearing on many of the tearooms mentioned in this book. Throughout this book I use the terms 'café,' 'tearoom' and 'coffee shop' interchangeably, partly because if somewhere has gone to the trouble of calling itself a coffee shop rather than a tearoom, I ought to respect its wishes at least some of the time. Also, I enjoy exercising the freedom I have to press into use whichever word or phrase takes my fancy at a given moment.

Why these particular tearooms?

Every tearoom in this book has made me feel special while I've been there. Some of them are immediately impressive on entering, while others are more self-effacing, subtle and quietly confident in their welcome. Whatever the style, décor, size or layout, I have found every tearoom featured here to have its own interesting atmosphere, which for some reason or other (detailed in each entry) has made a favourable impression on me. It may be that some of my choices appeal to you more than others, but I hope you will agree with me that there are some real gems to be found in these areas, and that every tearoom in this book has something to recommend it.

Although I am very enthusiastic about every tearoom in this guide, it's a good idea, as a friend once told me, to keep your expectations reasonably low so that you're constantly surprised and delighted by the good things that happen to you. That may seem an odd thing to say when, at the same time, I'm trying to promote these places, but I just don't want you to be disappointed. I once went so over-the-top telling my sister how fabulous one of these places was that her expectations were sky high and when she got there, she found it disappointing. Perhaps it would have paid off if I'd been a little less voluble in my praise, but then again perhaps not.

To make sure my reviews were up to date and I wasn't biased by my feelings on one particular day, I have visited each tearoom in the book this year, 2012, on at least two occasions (usually many more) before including it in this guidebook. I have been enjoying tearooms all over the place for years, and quite a few of my long-term favourites are featured in this book. I'm sure that, in some cases, the familiarity of some of these places has added to my enjoyment of them, but before I included any tearoom in this guide I ran it past my two most delightful assistants (see **My delightful assistants** on page 19), who tend to keep their feet on the ground far better than I do. If it passed muster with me and got the thumbs up from them, in it went.

A note about temperature

I deliberately focus on positive aspects in my reviews and sometimes there are down sides about a place that might be enough to put other people off. One particular issue in Scotland is the temperature and there are times when I've felt a bit on the cold side, even in some of my favourite tearooms, and in that case I would warn you to always make sure you're well dressed for the weather and if you're at all doubtful about it, it's always a good idea to take an extra layer. I virtually never drive off without a hat, scarf, gloves, jacket and a pair of woolly tights in my car whatever the time of year, because you just never know and I like to be cosy. This business about temperature is, however, a very personal one, and that's why I don't mention it in any of my reviews. I've felt too cold in a place and been with someone who felt it was exactly the right temperature, and vice versa, so there's no telling what any one individual may find comfortable on a particular day.

A note about perfection

As close as some of those in this book come to it, in my opinion, no tearoom is entirely perfect. Like a good friend, even my favourite tearoom might have its own idiosyncrasies that would put someone else off. Like good friends, however, we accept each other's faults and failings and embrace the joyful friendship regardless. All I hope for is that you find something pleasurable in the tearooms I recommend, and with any luck you may even love them as much as I do.

A note about scones

It seems to have become quite popular in recent years for some tearooms to warm their scones in a microwave oven. I can only assume that they do this in an attempt to make the scone taste freshly baked. Where this falls down, however, is that a microwaved scone loses both its flavour and texture and becomes, to my mind at least, considerably degraded. Maybe you like having your scone microwaved, in which case this will not trouble you at all, but for anyone like me, who doesn't, I would advise you to check about scone warming when placing your order. There are many tearooms that would never dream of doing this, but I've often been surprised by an otherwise excellent tearoom bringing me a microwaved scone. There are even some of those in this book, but it could be that some staff do it and some don't, and it just depends on who serves you on the day.

My opinion on microwaving scones is this. If the scone is fresh then microwaving it is tantamount to a criminal act, and if it's not fresh then microwaving it isn't going to make it fresh. Even if a tearoom is selling yesterday's scones (not advisable, but I accept that it happens), I would rather have it cold and slightly dried out than microwaved, warm and chewy.

If the reason for microwaving is to thaw out frozen scones, I would urge tearooms to take scones out of the freezer the night before, to allow full thawing by morning.

If you really want your old scone warm, I would suggest toasting it instead of zapping it with microwaves. I do this with my own scones at home when they're a day old and, although it can create a bit of trouble in terms of crumbs stuck in the toaster and the scone falling to pieces, I think it's worth it to bring back some crispness and make the old scone more appealing. Perhaps you strongly disagree with me on the microwaving subject, and if you do then I humbly apologise, but since I have the floor here I wanted to say my piece.

My delightful assistants

During my research visits to these tearooms, I have often had the company of some delightful assistants, notably my tea-loving mother and, occasionally, my father, other members of my family, or some of my dear chums, to assist me in this task. I have found that my mum, quite apart from being lovely company, is a delightful assistant who has very helpfully contributed another opinion and has often commented on points that I would have missed myself. She is a fellow lover of fine tearooms, and always keen to visit a new one, and I am indebted to her for her help and enthusiasm.

Website updates

As is the nature of things, tearooms come and go, and ownership/management changes, so that there are bound to be some details that quickly go out of date. It is my intention that the publishing blog for Teacups Press will feature updates on major changes as soon as I become aware of them, and I will do my best to keep this up-to-date. In addition, this blog hosts photos of all the tearooms featured in this guidebook. The blog address is:

www.teacupspress.com

There is also the blog that started alongside this book, where you can find regular posts on tearoom visits and associated witterings:

www.lornastearoomdelights.com

Phone numbers

If you're very keen to visit one particular tearoom, I would recommend phoning ahead to check that they are going to be open. A phone number is given for every tearoom featured. (From outside the UK, add 44 to the start of the number and miss off the first 0.)

How to use the guidebook

The tearooms have been arranged with reference to
the map on the inside back cover and are listed on the
Contents page (page 5) in the order that they appear
throughout the book. Every tearoom in the book has a
section to itself, with useful information in a box at the
end of each review. The boxed information is laid out
under the following nine headings:

Contact   address, phone number, and website
address if there is one

Location   basic local directions, to be used in
conjunction with a road map unless you
know the area well

Open   opening hours, sometimes different in
summer and winter, or on different days
of the week, please also see **Opening
hours** on the next page

Access   information about wheelchair accessibility

Children   availability of seating for children

Payment   whether or not the tearoom takes credit
(and debit) cards

Parking   suggested nearby parking options

Size   please see **Size** on the next page

Alcohol   licensed or not licensed to sell alcohol

The things I've written about each tearoom are a result of how the tearoom has struck me. I haven't included everything about a place, and indeed I may have missed out something that you feel should have been highlighted. What I hope to achieve in each review is to give a flavour of the tearoom, and leave you to add your own observations when you visit.

Opening hours

Opening hours do change from year to year and from season to season, and in most – perhaps all – cases the tearooms will be closed on 25 and 26 December, and perhaps 1 and 2 January as well. If you happen to be wanting to visit on these dates I would most definitely advise phoning ahead to check if they're open. (If I'm at all doubtful I often give the tearoom a quick ring at any time of year, to avoid disappointment).

Some tearooms may stop serving 30 minutes before closing time, so if they close at 5:00pm, last orders will be at 4:30pm (this is usually for food, rather than just a drink, but in most cases it's a good idea to arrive at least half an hour before they close, for the best tearoom experience).

Size

The approximate number of people the tearoom can accommodate, was counted by me for each tearoom. Rather than give the precise number of seats, I have used the following categorisation:

Small = seating fewer than 20 people

Medium = seating 20ish to 40ish

Large = seating considerably more than 40 (may include outdoor seating)

Coffee

The description 'Italian style coffees' covers all espresso-based coffees such as cappuccino, Americano and latte, as distinct from filter coffee or that served in a cafetiere (French press).

Tea

In many cases in these tearooms the tea comes by way of a teabag. If there is leaf tea available, I have tried to include that information (my apologies to any tearooms I neglect to draw attention to in this matter). While some purists may shun anything other than leaf tea (and I can understand the preference, leaf tea does often have more flavour), I must say I have had some truly excellent tea from teabags. I suppose it all depends on the quality of what's in the bag.

On the subject of leaf tea, it's such a pleasure to discover a tearoom that does offer leaf tea that I hope this is something that will increase in availability. I know there are people who are avidly campaigning for more leaf tea in tearooms, and I do agree with them that it's great to get it. For one thing, there is an enormous variety of leaf teas available (by way of black, green, white and yellow teas, quite apart from the myriad herbal options) and you rarely see a true sample of the huge range of options. On the other hand, the tea choices in most tearooms are vastly improved from what they were only a few years ago.

I can think of one tearoom in another area of Scotland that serves an excellent range of leaf teas, and I always enjoy going there and sampling a different tea. It's known for the choices of high quality teas and this draws in dedicated tea drinkers, as well as regular punters, so it's a win-win situation. It also gets a lot of other things right, with the china, ambience, cakes, etc. and is quite rightly a very successful place. However, I can also think of a tearoom that serves excellent leaf tea but lets the customers down in every other area, and so despite the undeniable quality of the tea, I wouldn't choose to go back there. My point is, just serving leaf tea isn't enough; it's an excellent additional feature, but it isn't – in my opinion, at least – the be all and end all. Again though, I must reiterate that this is simply my opinion and you may think differently about it. If you're a coffee drinker, I daresay none of this will bother you in the slightest and you'll be wondering what all the fuss is about, but the fact is tea drinkers can be a pretty picky bunch (myself included, and of course I fiercely defend this pedantry).

Public Transport

Public transport is available to some of these tearooms, but in many cases outside of Perth and Dundee this tends to be limited to infrequent local bus services. The train network is not extensive in the areas covered, although some small towns, such as Arbroath, do have railway stations. Information about public transport is not included in this guidebook but there is a national website dedicated to the subject that allows you to plan journeys all over Scotland (this information can also be obtained by phone on 0871 200 2233):

www.travelinescotland.com

Treats

Up in the north-western corner of Perthshire, a long trout-filled loch sparkles between Bridge of Gaur to the west and Kinloch Rannoch to the east. At the eastern end, on the main street in the sleepy little village of Kinloch Rannoch, sits a surprisingly modern and excellent tearoom called Treats. I wouldn't have expected such a small place off the beaten track to have this sort of tearoom. I might have anticipated something much more old-fashioned, perhaps with lace curtains in the windows and a slight air of neglect inside, not doing much business and having become a part of the scenery, cobwebs and all. Treats is very far removed from this vision.

When you enter the tearoom you find yourself in an attractive open plan area that combines gift shop and café, with a cake counter and till at the far end of the room. In the middle of this room is a long table, which sometimes has a couple of newspapers on it. The situation of this central table with chairs down either side makes me think of a farmhouse kitchen, and its location with one end facing out to the front door produces a very welcoming, homely feel as you walk into the room. At the back of this room, through a doorway (without a door) to the left, is the Art Room, where some local artwork is displayed around the walls. There are more tables and chairs here, and a few beautifully striped easy chairs. There is some seating at picnic tables outside across the road as well, if you care to dine *al fresco*.

I think the food selection is very good, particularly for a place so far away from the nearest town (Aberfeldy and Pitlochry are roughly equidistant, being about 40 minutes' drive away), and the portions are generous.

There are always one or two freshly made soups of the day, which are served in large bowls that seem to me to be almost bottomless, paninis, rolls and special mixed platters, which include locally sourced meat and fish from the Rannoch Smokery along the road. Although there is a set menu, the friendly staff are very amenable to any changes you might like to request. There is also a children's option, which consists of sandwiches and fruit, and they do quite a brisk trade in takeaways. If the sun's shining, this is the perfect place to stock up for a picnic along the lochside.

The cake selection consists of a number of traybakes, sponge cakes, muffins and scones, most of which are baked on the premises. There is a variety of tea and coffee (and very good hot chocolate) on offer, the coffee being Italian style, and all hot beverages are Fairtrade. They also give out loyalty cards, which entitle you to a free hot drink after purchasing 8. The gift shop sells a range of interesting and locally produced craft items, including paintings, wood carvings and framed photographs, as well as stocking items from farther afield, such as toiletries, cards, mugs and jewellery. Leaflets are available in the gift shop giving details of other local places of interest.

Treats – useful information

Contact	The Square, Kinloch Rannoch, PH16 5PF Tel: 01882 632333
Location	on the main street in Kinloch Rannoch, the B846
Open	every day 10:00am – 5:00pm
Access	wheelchair accessible, with accessible toilet
Children	high chairs available
Payment	credit cards accepted
Parking	free on-street parking in the village
Size	medium
Alcohol	café not licensed

The Watermill

The smell of freshly brewed coffee, the clink of cutlery on plates, exposed stone walls, arched windows, beautiful lighting, world music playing softly in the background, and shelves full of interesting tomes. That's what you get when you visit The Watermill; it is a veritable feast for eyes, mind and tastebuds.

The building was constructed in 1825 as a working watermill, but has now been transformed into a fantastic bookshop, tearoom and gallery on three levels. It's the largest bookshop in the rural Scottish highlands and has been voted "best independent bookshop in the UK." It's certainly one of my favourite bookshops anywhere, and the café has an excellent selection of unusual leaf teas.

On the lower floor is the tearoom, along with travel books and maps. The main bookshop occupies the middle floor, and up at the top floor is an art gallery. I think of a visit to the Watermill as a triple treat: tasty morsels, followed by books, followed by artworks. That's the order I do it in, starting at the bottom of the building and working my way up.

It can be a very busy place, this, although it never feels hectic to me because it has a relaxed and easy-going atmosphere. The café contains sofas and armchairs with coffee tables, as well as dining tables and chairs, and offers light lunches and a selection of tempting cakes. As tearooms go, the menu is fairly small, but the quality is high and the ambience is wonderful.

Savoury options comprise soups served with organic bread, and ciabattas with interesting fillings, e.g. goat's cheese with honey, beetroot and baby gem lettuce. Ciabattas come with a side salad. There are usually several sponge cake options, including a gluten-free cake, croissants and biscuits. Some of the cakes are slightly unusual, e.g. chocolate, hazelnut and banana, but always delicious, in my experience (I especially like their chocolate cake, which isn't always available, but when it is I find it very tempting and it goes down a treat with a pot of Russian Caravan tea).

As mentioned, the tea choices are excellent, some of them being exotic leaf teas served in cast iron Japanese teapots with little handle-less cups, e.g. Jasmine, Green Tea Sencha and White Monkey, as well as more commonly available black teas. The coffees are Italian style or cafetiere and are also very good (quite strong, too, but you can opt for one shot instead of two, if you so desire). You can also have decaffeinated coffee, and choose to have semi-skimmed or soya milk, if preferred. Both tea and coffee are Fairtrade. They also do a very good-looking hot chocolate that I've yet to try, as well as organic juices and smoothies.

A fantastic renovation job has been done on the building, creating a very inviting, and almost magical, place to browse and enjoy books and artwork. Even when I've only popped in here for a quick snack, I don't think I've ever left without one of their lovely paper bags containing one or two book purchases. For me, and I'm sure for many others, this is the perfect shopping environment and, as if I needed any lure to revisit, they have a loyalty card that entitles you to a free hot drink after purchasing 7.

The Watermill – useful information

Contact	Mill Street, Aberfeldy, PH15 2BG Tel: 01887 822896 www.aberfeldywatermill.com
Location	off the main street in Aberfeldy (A827), signposted in the town
Open	Monday to Saturday 10:00am – 5:00pm (5.30pm in the summer) Sunday 11:00am – 5:00pm
Access	wheelchair accessible via a ramp at the back of the building, with accessible toilet
Children	high chairs available
Payment	credit cards accepted
Parking	there is a car park at the back of the building, and free on-street parking in Aberfeldy
Size	large (including outdoor seating)
Alcohol	café not licensed

Between the café and the shop there is a small chocolate museum, detailing the history and methods of chocolate making, and there are four steps up to the shop from here. A disabled hoist is provided, so that wheelchair users can move between the shop and café without having to go outside. (The front door of the shop is at street level and the café entrance is also on the level, but the hoist is required due to a difference in ground level over the whole area.) If you're at all interested in chocolate, you'll want to have a look at the superb creations on sale in the shop. There is a chocolate counter full of delicious award winning individual chocolates, and there are various bars and packets of different chocolates and cocoa powders for sale.

At time of publication, they are busy installing a chocolate viewing area, where you will be able to watch the chocolate being made.

Legends – useful information

Contact
Legends, Grandtully, Perthshire, PH9 0PL
Tel: 01887 840775
www.legendsofgrandtully.com

Location
on the main street in Grandtully, 5 miles
northeast of the small town of Aberfeldy and
about 10 miles southwest of Pitlochry

Open
every day 10:00am – 5:00pm
(except 24 & 25 December, and 1 January)
winter opening times 11.00am – 4.00pm
(26 December until mid-March)

Access
shop and café wheelchair accessible but with
four steps between them and hoist enabling
access between the two, accessible toilet in
the café

Children
one high chair available

Payment
credit cards accepted

Parking
plenty free parking in café's own car park

Size
large (including outdoor seating)

Alcohol
café not licensed

Kirkmichael village shop

The village of Kirkmichael is very small and yet it houses a most remarkable village shop, which is also a café, a post office, an off licence and a fuel station (during shop opening hours). It used to be a car showroom, and one of the interesting (and well disguised) features of the tearoom is that part of the floor slopes downwards, where the garage ramp used to be. It's as well to be aware of this when ordering beverages as one or two of the tables can be a bit rocky.

The Kirkmichael village shop might seem rather a strange choice for a guidebook to tearooms, because as a tearoom it is pretty basic, very small and is really just an add-on to the shop. However, it's included here because the whole place is so full of interest and I always enjoy coming here.

The small tearoom area is a quiet and relaxing place and, although the menu sticks to the basics, hot snacks and rolls are made to order and I've very much enjoyed both lunch and afternoon tea here. I've found the tea in particular to be very good, perhaps because it's made from freshly boiled water in a kettle rather than from an urn or similar constantly boiling hot water supply. The coffee is filter, unless you want decaf, in which case it's instant (I had a mug of their decaf once and thoroughly enjoyed it). Hot food consists of soup, bacon rolls (on fresh white fluffy rolls) and toasties. They also stock freshly baked croissants and other pastries, and have a choice of traybakes, biscuits and cakes, lovingly home-baked by the ladies of the village.

There is a lot to look at while you wait for your tea or coffee to cool down, and there are complimentary newspapers for perusing in the café, as well as various free tourist leaflets to browse through. The shop stocks a quite astonishing selection of items, including local produce, speciality foodstuffs, car paraphernalia (screenwash, oil, etc.), manila envelopes, string, woolly hats, keyrings, maps, cards, locally made craft items and much more besides. It is also the village hub, where locals come in to use the post office, buy odds and ends and have a wee chat with the staff. In some places this could make an outsider feel a little uncomfortable, but because Kirkmichael is a popular area for walkers, they're used to visitors and I have always been made to feel very welcome here.

Taking tea in their little tearoom area, I feel absorbed into the community. I always find it a fascinating place to rest the weary legs after a walk, stoke up the boiler for a bit of exercise or just pop into during a journey. Wi-fi is available and the shop contains an ATM (there is a charge for transactions).

Kirkmichael Village Shop – useful information

Contact Main Street, Kirkmichael, PH10 7NT
Tel: 01250 881272
www.kirkmichael-village-shop.co.uk

Location on the A924, in the main street through
Kirkmichael, roughly 12 miles equidistant
from Pitlochry and Blairgowrie

Open Monday to Saturday 8:00am – 5:00pm
(winter) 8:00am – 6:00pm (summer)
Sunday 10:00am – 2:00pm (winter)
9:00am – 5:00pm (summer)

Access shop and café wheelchair accessible, toilets
not accessible

Children high chairs not available

Payment credit cards accepted

Parking space for 2 or 3 cars right outside the shop,
free on-street parking throughout the village

Size small

Alcohol café not licensed

Peel Farm

I've been popping in and out of Peel Farm for
several years and have seen quite a few changes in
the café over that time. I'm delighted to report that I
think it's now at the best it's ever been, under new
management since 2011. I think they've got the
homespun farmhouse feel, mixed with the modern
desire for comfort and nice things, down to a tee, and
not surprisingly it has become a very popular place for
a day out. As a business, Peel Farm has been on the
go for 30 years and, as well as being a working mixed
(arable and livestock) farm, comprises the café, a
farm shop and a craft shop

The main room of the café (there is also a
conservatory, open in the warmer weather) has dark
wooden beams in the ceiling, and a cosy atmosphere
(on cold days, with the fire lit at one end of the room,
you will probably want to linger here for some
considerable time). They've fairly packed the tables in,
and although this could make moving around slightly
difficult, I like the sociable ambience they've achieved.
It doesn't seem as if you're cheek by jowl with other
diners, but it does feel as if you could lean over and
have a little chat with a neighbour if you fancied it.

The cake counter and till are at one end of the
room, opposite the door into the café. This means that
as soon as you step through the front door you're

confronted with a fabulous array of treats to lure you in (it works for me every time).

The cake selection is very tempting, including some truly wonderful large sponge cakes, traybakes and large scones. On at least two occasions when I've been there, just as I was finishing my meal, a new, big, nicely decorated sponge cake was brought out of the kitchen. My timing is obviously not very good because it has pained me to see these big newly baked cakes arriving when I'm already full up.

Tasty savoury options include sandwiches, toasties, soup, paninis, baked potatoes and special hot dishes of the day, e.g. lasagne. There are also homemade rustic Peel pies, with a variety of fillings. The tea and Fairtrade coffee are very good, and interesting leaf and teabag tea is available (both black and herbal). There are various cold drinks, along with a milkshake menu from which you can create your own concoction.

Beyond the café, there is plenty to look at and enjoy, including the craft and gift shop, farm shop, and, across the road at the entrance, a duck pond full  of lovely waterfowl. The craft shop contains gifts, food, clothing and antique furniture, and the separate farm shop is stocked with a range of local and national produce. If you have a moment before or after your refreshments, you might like to take a peek at the mosaics outside the school next-door to Peel Farm.

Peel Farm – useful information

Contact	Peel Farm, Lintrathen, By Kirriemuir, Angus, DD8 5JJ Tel: 01575 560205 www.peelfarm.com
Location	near Loch of Lintrathen, about 6 miles north-east of Alyth (off the B954) and about 9 miles west of Kirriemuir (off the B951)
Open	every day 10:00am – 5:00pm 1 March to 23 December, closed 24 December to 5 January, open Friday, Saturday and Sunday 10:00am – 5:00pm early January to end February
Access	wheelchair accessible, with accessible toilet next to the café
Children	five high chairs available
Payment	credit cards accepted
Parking	large car park in front of the café and shop, with overflow area next to it
Size	large (including outdoor seating)
Alcohol	café not licensed

Edzell Tweedie

The attractive village of Edzell has a few shops and a hotel, but the Tweedie Coffee House feels to me like the hub of the community. I've often heard locals exchanging a bit of village gossip over their coffees, or with the assistants at the till.

As I sat at a table in here one day, enjoying a cafetiere of excellent decaf coffee and a lemon coconut slice, I made some notes about how the Tweedie made me feel. I jotted down four words that summed up my feelings and which, whenever I think of the Tweedie, vividly remind me of being there: warm, light, quiet and comfortable. I can't guarantee that you will feel all of these things yourself, but on the number of occasions I've visited, they've always seemed very apt to me.

There's something quietly relaxing about the Tweedie, and just thinking about it as I write this makes me feel calm and peaceful. I don't know how this works, and why it should be that some places seem to have a particularly relaxing atmosphere but, like the Parrot Café in Dundee, the Edzell Tweedie is a place I come out of feeling noticeably more serene than when I went in.

I particularly like the cake counter in here, because it's an old-fashioned glass affair with lots of tasty cakes and traybakes displayed on shelves behind glass, and a selection of different scones on top of the counter. The delicious scones are baked on the premises using Perthshire flour, and in addition to the more traditional flavours they sometimes have interesting selections, such as lemon and poppy seed. Both the tea and the coffee are very good, and they have a nice choice of Australian Bundaberg sparkling juices, including lemon, lime and bitters, and peachee, as well as the signature ginger beer.

Hot food includes hearty homemade soups (served with award winning Aberfeldy oatcakes, soda bread, a roll, or a cheese scone), bacon rolls, toasted bagels, paninis and baked potatoes. There are also daily specials chalked up on a blackboard (which often include a comforting hot pudding of some description, e.g. apple crumble and custard). The chicken and eggs used in the tearoom are all free range and locally produced, and if you have any special dietary requirements they offer to try and fulfil your request.

If you choose to sit on the sofa, you'll find a big stack of newspapers and magazines within easy reach next to one end of it, and there's plenty to look at in the shop adjoining the tearoom. The shop sells local farm produce, a few clothes, cards, jewellery and a range of other gift items, all arranged in an open-plan layout.

Edzell Tweedie – useful information

Contact	1 Dunlappie Road, Edzell, By Brechin, DD9 7UB Tel: 01356 648348
Location	on the corner of Dunlappie Road and the B966 (the main road through Edzell), about 6 miles north of Brechin
Open	Monday to Saturday 10:00am – 5:00pm Sunday 12:00am – 5:00pm
Access	wheelchair accessible, with accessible toilet
Children	high chairs available
Payment	credit cards accepted, but a small charge is made for amounts under £10.00
Parking	free on-street parking outside the Tweedie, throughout Edzell
Size	medium
Alcohol	cafe licensed

Palmerstons

Some time, you might find yourself in the pretty village of Dunkeld, ambling along the main street being delighted by the interesting independent shops on offer and feeling a tad peckish. If, as you stroll towards Palmerston's, you peep in and happen to see an empty table and wonder if you should take advantage of this happy occurrence, my advice would be to slide in there post haste and claim it, before someone else snaps it up.

I've queued for a table at Palmerston's on a number of occasions (usually at the busy lunchtime period) and often wished the walls were expandable, so that a few more tables could be fitted in. It's not always hectically busy, but I mention this just to prepare you in case you're thinking of turning up on the off chance for lunch one day (they don't take bookings).

Lunch at Palmerston's is certainly worth parting with your cash for, but I like to shimmy in here mid-late morning for a lovely pot of tea or a cup of coffee and one of their excellent triangular scones. They often have four different scone varieties, and I've been fortunate enough to try a number of splendidly interesting flavours. They do sometimes sell out of these wonderful confections, which is another good reason for calling in late morning, but if that's the case, or indeed you fancy something else, there's no

46

shortage of wonderful cakey choices. Before I move onto other edibles, however, I must highlight the jam. When you order one of their marvellous scones, it comes with a little bowl of home-made preserve, and whatever the flavour on the day, I've always been delighted with it. My favourite is possibly the apple and kiwi, but I remember a rhubarb one which was also exquisite.

As for other cakes, every one I've had here has exceeded my expectations, from the superb rock buns, to the intensely chocolatey rocky road, the moist and moreish tea loaf and the fluffy and delicious sponge cakes. They do excellent muffins, too. I think Palmerston's must have one of the most appetising cake choices, for my palate at least, anywhere in Perthshire.

In addition to all these cakey delights, savoury food includes soup, sandwiches and baguettes, baked potatoes and haggis. There are also children's 'bizzi bags' which contain a sandwich, sweet treat, drink, puzzles and games. The standard tea is a nice flavourful pot, and there are various herbal and fruit teas as well. The coffee is Italian style, and they do a luxuriously rich hot chocolate with marshmallows and chocolate on the top. They also have a small selection of alcoholic beverages, including wine, beer and cider.

They have a loyalty card that gives you a free coffee when you've bought 9 (tea not included).

Palmerston's – useful information

Contact   20 Atholl Street, Dunkeld, PH8 0AJ
Tel: 01350 7272315
www.palmerstons.eu

Location   about halfway along the main street
through Dunkeld

Open   Monday to Saturday: 10:00am – 4:15pm
Sunday 11:00am – 4:15pm

Access   wheelchair accessible, with accessible
toilet (because the café is quite small tables
are fairly tightly packed)

Children   high chairs available

Payment credit cards not accepted

Parking   free on-street parking in the main street,
two pay car parks, one at either end of the
village

Size   medium

Alcohol   cafe licensed

✾ Bradberries ✾

Bradberries is a family run tearoom that first opened for business in 2011 but has already become well established and well loved in Blairgowrie. There are large windows at the front of the tearoom facing south that let in plenty of sunshine on a sunny day. If you're sitting in one of the window seats on such an occasion you can easily imagine you're in some Mediterranean hotspot.

The interior design is attractive, with a lot of fresh, clean white as well as some bold dark red walls. They've deliberately opted for a 'berry' theme, wanting to celebrate the fact that Blairgowrie is known for its soft fruit farms. The story of how they came up with the name 'Bradberries' is framed on one wall and makes for interesting reading.

If Blairgowrie is enjoying any sun at all, Bradberries seems to scoop it up and fill the room with it, but for those colder wintery days, there is a welcome fireplace with a wood-effect fire inside it, and logs piled up at the sides, creating a cosy and homely feel.

When I started writing this entry I noted that there were easy chairs and low coffee tables in the windows, and a sofa at the back of the room with a coffee table, but I've since noticed that furniture likes to move around the room in Bradberries, and so I'd better not commit myself to the layout in this review. In any case, there is a choice of seating, and I'm always interested to see where the chairs have moved to between visits.

The tables and chairs are of plain, pale coloured, wood and some of the chairs have cushions on them. There is also one very sweet child size table with two little chairs and a box of toys for children to play with. In fine weather you can sit outside at aluminium tables on the pavement and watch the world go by, and this appears to be very popular.

Inside, the tables have fresh flowers on them, as well as salt and pepper grinders, and a bowl of rough brown and white sugar cubes with a set of tongs. Menus are brought to the tables by the friendly waitresses.

The menu includes a good range of cakes and scones (the fruit scones are excellent), with a variety of sponge cakes, traybakes and fruit loaf. Every day there is a soup of the day and the menu includes breakfast fare such as bacon rolls, as well as toasties, paninis, sandwiches and salads.

Coffee is available in a cafétiere or Italian style, and the decaffeinated coffee is very good. The teapots are delivered to the table complete with knitted teacosies. They also serve afternoon tea on tiered plates, and have several tiered cake stands on display, as well as some lovely china teacups and saucers.

Bradberries – useful information

Contact	5 High Street, Blairgowrie, PH10 6ET Tel: 07525 465970
Location	on the main street through Blairgowrie, on the left hand side as you travel east, just before the bend in the road changes from the High Street into Allan Street
Open	Monday to Saturday 9:30am – 4:00pm
Access	wheelchair accessible, with accessible toilet
Children	high chairs available, with one child-size table and chairs
Payment	credit cards not accepted
Parking	free on-street parking outside the café, for up to 30 minutes, longer stay pay car parks behind the shops across the road
Size	medium
Alcohol	cafe not licensed

The Wee Coffee Shop

The Wee Coffee Shop has won local awards for its lunches and service, and I think it also deserves an award for cleanliness. I don't think I've ever had such consistently shiny cutlery anywhere else, and I'm always impressed by how neat, tidy and well kept the whole place is. It's not just the cutlery that gleams either, it must have the sparkliest flooring I've ever seen in a bathroom.

It's always reassuring to find an eating establishment that takes such good care of its hygiene, and it's the same with the plates and cups, all very clean and shiny and a pleasure to eat and drink from.

The food consists of hot filled rolls, paninis (with quite an extensive choice of fillings), sandwiches and soups. The soups, interestingly, can be served in a bread bowl, if desired. I haven't had the soup in bread option here, but I did have it somewhere else once and it fairly floored me. If you have a good appetite and need something filling, I think soup in a loaf of bread could be just the choice for you.

The room is pleasingly light and nicely laid out, with some paintings by local artists for sale on the walls. The paintings are very well priced, and although not done by professional artists, have a certain charm and character. I have twice been tempted by paintings in here, one of what seemed to me to be a miniature schnauzer and another of a highland cow with calf. Both of them made me smile, and whatever your view on the artistic merit of the work, I think they do add something positive to the ambience.

Encouraging the artists of tomorrow, children are welcomed with a little pot of crayons and some sheets to colour in.

The coffee is cafetiere or Italian style and there are some very nice leaf teas. There are also Sweetbird flavoured syrups that can be added to drinks (these are apparently the only such syrups to be endorsed for vegan diets).

The traybakes here are particularly good and I think the coconut and lemon slice is probably the best I've had anywhere (in the interests of scientific research I've been trying them out wherever I can).

There's a very good view of the street from inside, with the café being right next to a junction, and the traffic problems that frequently ensue at this point in the town make for quite entertaining viewing. Best of all, the good soundproofing means that the noise of the street is kept outside and you can barely hear it in the café.

I've been collecting loyalty cards for tearooms for years (unfortunately, I often forget to use them), and I think The Wee Coffee Shop's deal must be the best yet; when you've bought 5 hot drinks you get 1 free.

The Wee Coffee Shop – useful information

Contact 1 Allan Street, Blairgowrie, PH10 6AB
Tel: 07919 341870

Location on the main street through Blairgowrie,
near the Leslie Street/Wellmeadow junction

Open Tuesday to Saturday 10:00am – 4:30pm

Access wheelchair accessible, with accessible
toilet

Children high chair available

Payment credit cards not accepted

Parking free on-street parking at nearby
Wellmeadow and Leslie Street for up to 30
mins, longer stay pay car parks behind
shops across the road

Size medium

Alcohol cafe not licensed

Cardeans

If you happen to be in the area of Meigle looking for a delicious breakfast or brunch late morning I would highly recommend popping into Cardeans. This eatery is signed up to the Perthshire Breakfast Initiative, a scheme that supports local businesses by sourcing at least 50% of their breakfast products locally, and they cook their delicious breakfasts to order. You can choose from a full Scottish breakfast, scrambled eggs, bacon rolls, etc., or opt for just a couple of slices of very nice toast with marmalade or jam.

Cardeans is attached to Mervat's Gallery, and the walls are decorated with pictures for sale, some of which are quite large framed paintings.

In addition to breakfasts, hot food includes baked potatoes, toasties and soup, and an impressive selection of hot specials, often including a vegetarian option. A traditional Scottish high tea is served through the week from 12.00am – 4.00pm and on Sundays from 4.00pm – 6.00pm. The high tea consists of a selection of main courses, including a vegetarian option, followed by homemade cakes and scones, and tea or coffee. If you're just after a snack, there are various traybakes, scones and sponges on offer, along with a variety of teas, and both cafétiere and Italian style coffees.

There is a lot of natural light from the large windows at the front of the building, and a log fire is sometimes lit in a stove at the back of the café. The tables and chairs are of dark wood, with the chairs having padded seats. The seating is all contained in one large room, with the back and side walls painted in a dark red colour. I think the warm colour and choice of furniture works well with the large amount of natural light. With quite a high ceiling and spaciously laid out tables, it could easily feel a bit empty or stark, but in fact the décor gives the whole place a cosy feel. Vases of fresh flowers and a few large pot plants add to the ambience, and I think the room has been very well designed.

There is usually gentle music on in the background, but it's played quietly enough to be unobtrusive, and there is a toy box for children.

Despite the provisions for younger diners, whenever I've been in Cardeans I've felt as if I'm giving myself a bit of a grown-up treat. It has a restauranty elegance to it that makes it quite different from most of the other entries in this book. I deliberately haven't included eateries that I consider to be more restaurants than tearooms, but Cardeans manages to capture that middle ground, somewhere between a tearoom and a restaurant and I think they pull it off perfectly.

Cardeans – useful information

Contact   Alyth Road, Meigle, PH12 8RP
Tel: 01828 640740
www.cardeans.com

Location   on the main road through Meigle (A94) near the west end of the village

Open   Tuesday to Saturday 10.00am – 5.00pm, Sunday 10.00am – 6.30pm (with high tea from 4.00pm) (closed Monday)

Access   wheelchair accessible, with accessible toilet

Children   high chairs available

Payment   credit cards accepted

Parking   large gravelled car park outside café and art gallery

Size   medium

Alcohol   café licensed

Joinery Café

Some years ago the Joinery Café building housed a joiner's shop, hence the name. The original joinery dated back to the 19th Century and when I first started visiting it as a café (in the 21st Century), there was a sense of this connection to its carpentry past, with a few joinery tools around the room. It has since been revamped and turned into an attractive combination of gift shop and café. The joinery tools seem to have gone but a lot of interesting things have replaced them, including an impressive selection of mirrors for sale.

In addition to radiators round the walls, the room is heated by a large central fire from which a pyramidal brick chimney steps up to the ceiling. There are sofas and coffee tables next to the fire, and on a cold day these areas provide a cosy nest of warmth from which it can be quite difficult to extricate yourself. If I call in here late morning and order one of their very cheesy cheese scones or, if I fancy something sweeter, a piece of delightful tiffin, I can happily lose myself in my snack and a nice pot of tea, dreaming of days gone by when the room would have been filled with a resiny smell and sawdust carpeted the wooden floorboards. I like the idea of a joinery being transformed into a café, I feel it's what the wood would have wanted.

A good selection of café fare is on offer here, including soup, baked potatoes, paninis, toasties, bagels and sandwiches, and there is quite a variety of traybakes and other sweet treats. One very cold morning my mum and I called in here, and I had a real hankering for tea and toast. The obliging staff provided us with this and, to our delight, brought along lemon and lime marmalade, too. It was years since I'd had this marmalade and it brought back happy memories of my childhood.

As well as the plethora of interesting mirrors for sale, there are a few lamps, cards, buddhas and other ornaments. It might be that they don't always have the same selection of things for sale, but on the previous few occasions I've been here I've been very taken with one particular item. I think it's a draught excluder and is all joined together, but it looks like six toy dogs in a row. This very one may not be there any more, I don't know, but I have a photograph of one that shows these six dogs with the fourth one looking very shy hiding beneath one of its own and one of its

neighbour's ears. I thought it was very sweet.

Considering its size, the village of Meigle is very well served with tearooms, having both the Joinery Café and Cardeans open for business very close to each other. And not only does it have two tearooms, but both of them happen to be, in my opinion, above average.

Joinery Café – useful information

Contact   The Square, Meigle, Blairgowrie,
             PH12 8RN
             Tel: 01828 640717
             www.meiglecoffeeshop.co.uk

Location   on the main road through Meigle (A94),
             next to the Spar shop

Open   Monday to Saturday 9:00am – 4.15pm
             (closed Tuesday)
             Sunday 10:00am – 4.15pm

Access   wheelchair accessible, accessible toilet

Children   high chairs available

Payment   credit cards accepted

Parking   free parking in the café's own car park,
             additional free parking on-street in Meigle

Size   large

Alcohol   café not licensed

Trumperton Forge

Trumperton Forge Tearoom is a beautiful old stone building with a horse stable next-door, complete with horse, located in a tranquil and beautiful setting.

Inside, the tearoom is very attractive, with dark wooden beams against a white ceiling, exposed stone walls, a tiled floor and big windows with fine countryside views. As well as the dining tables and chairs, there are some chests of drawers and wooden dressers, which give the place a very comfortable farmhouse feel. All of the chairs (many of which are of a dainty wooden design) have cushions on them, and the wooden tables are the shiniest I've ever seen. I think they must have been varnished, because they positively gleam. Interestingly, all the tables are extendable, and some of them have been extended to seat 6, while others are in their more compact state and seat 2 or 4 customers.

At each place setting a teacup and a small tea knife are laid out, and a very handy glass full of napkins is available on every table. Near the door there is a wonderful selection of cakes and traybakes, with a choice of sponge cakes kept under glass cloches, and there are also scones and pancakes.

Savoury food includes of a choice of soups, toasties, baked potatoes, wraps and sandwiches.

There is a selection of teas, milkshakes and juices. Coffees are Italian style or cafetiere, including decaf which I've had and enjoyed.

The tearoom also sells various gift and craft items, including vases, picture frames, second-hand books and a few locally carved wooden pieces. Above the shop area, the rafters are decorated with rows of dried flowers hanging down.

One of the things that makes this place special is the location. Even if you're not actually seated at the window tables, you can still gaze out at a beautiful pastoral scene, with animals in the foreground and rolling hills behind. If it's fine enough you can sit outside at wooden picnic tables on a patio just outside the tearoom door, where a clematis is growing up and over a wooden trellis.

Before or after your refreshments, you might like to say hello to some of the aforementioned animals. There are different types of chickens wandering around the car park, and several hutches with rabbits in them. In a field over a fence there are several ducks, a large turkey, a donkey, a goat and some horses. They seem to be used to visitors and the turkey has certainly been very vocal when I've toddled over to see him. I thought at first that he was talking to me, but then I realised that every time one of the horses neighed the turkey responded, and vice versa.

Trumperton Forge – useful information

Contact	East Trumperton Farm, Letham, Forfar, Angus, DD8 2PA Tel: 01307 818325
Location	7 miles east of Forfar on the Mains of Balmadies road, near Letham
Open	Tuesday to Sunday 12:00am – 5:00pm (closed Monday)
Access	wheelchair accessible, with accessible toilet
Children	high chairs available
Payment	credit cards not accepted
Parking	plenty of free parking outside the tearoom in gravelled parking area
Size	large
Alcohol	café not licensed

Sugar and Spice is a building full of treats and goodies. When you first walk in, you're presented with a well-stocked sweet shop selling a large range of old-fashioned sweeties in jars. You then move on to a small gift shop area and farther into the very popular licensed café.

The main body of the café is housed in an inner room and a conservatory, and because it's so popular you may well find you have to wait for a table if you arrive at a busy time (booking ahead is recommended at lunchtime, and if you need a high chair I would definitely recommend reserving one because this place is very popular with babies who lunch).

There are many reasons for its popularity, chief of these being the excellent and extensive menu, which includes a fair number of fish dishes (the café used to be a fish shop – see the website for notes on its interesting history). If you like fish, I can recommend the fish here. I've had both the beer battered haddock and the deliciously tasty Arbroath smokie pâté and both were excellent.

There is a warm, cosy feel about the place, and something of a celebratory atmosphere over lunchtime, due to the inevitable buzz of conversation from the many diners. It feels almost as if you're sitting in someone's house attending some sort of community event, and although the noise level can be quite high it's not in the harsh clangy way you get when there are too many hard surfaces.

There are various places to sit, from the small area in the sweetie shop window to the decking area outside the back of the tearoom. The lighting is pleasant throughout, with a lot of natural light in the conservatory and soft spot-lighting inside. The friendly waitresses are dressed in black uniforms with old-fashioned white aprons and little white caps.

Leaf tea is served with willow-pattern china cups and ceramic teapots, and is very good. The coffees are Italian style. In addition to the many choices on the menu (including some good vegetarian options), there are daily specials such as carrot and courgette soup, haddock mornay, and a chocolate brownie served with hot chocolate sauce. There are also some enormous meringues, various cakes, muffins, traybakes and several choices of large gluten-free scone.

The tables are wooden, of various sizes, and mostly round in shape, seating anything from 2 to 8. Most of the chairs are dining chairs but there are also a few easy chairs. A paper napkin, tucked into one of the many different designs of napkin ring throughout the cafe, rests at each place setting.

Sugar and Spice – useful information

Contact   9-13 High Street, Arbroath, Angus, DD11 1BE
                 Tel: 01241 437500
                 www.sugarandspiceshop.co.uk

Location   to the east of the town centre, towards the
                 seaward end of the High Street

Open   Summer (mid-June to September, weather
                 dependent): Monday to Thursday 9.00am –
                 7.00pm, Friday 9.00am – 9.00pm, Saturday
                 10.00am – 9.00pm, Sunday 12.00am – 7.00pm
                 Winter (October to mid-June, weather
                 dependent): Monday to Thursday 10.00am –
                 5.00pm, Friday 10.00am – 9.00pm, Saturday
                 10.00am – 9.00pm, Sunday 12.00am – 7.00pm

Access   wheelchair accessible, with accessible toilet

Children   high chairs available

Payment   credit cards accepted

Parking   cafe's own car park round the back, as well as
                 plenty of free on-street parking in Arbroath

Size   large

Alcohol   café licensed

Gloagburn

Gloagburn farm shop and café is a great success story. It opened as a farm shop in 2003 and has gone from strength to strength, expanding and growing over the years. I honestly have no idea how many times I've enjoyed refreshments at Gloagburn but it's certainly well into double figures. I've had morning tea, lunch and afternoon tea here (not all on the same day) and it is one of the tearooms I visit regularly, all year round. The highlights for me are the location, only 3 miles from the outskirts of Perth, the consistent high quality of the tea and scones, the pleasant ambience, cleanliness, roomy toilets and relaxed atmosphere, not to mention the interesting farm shop which I like to mooch round after consuming some delicious food and drink in the café.

Loose leaf tea is served in very good quality stainless steel teapots that don't dribble, with milk in matching stainless steel jugs, and the tea and coffee cups are made of Highland Stoneware with a jolly sheep design, which always cheers me up. Although their lunchtime food is excellent, with interesting and appetising daily specials, my favourite time to visit is late morning, for tea and one of their marvellous fruit scones. The scones are always a decent size (quite large), crisp on the outside and soft and fluffy on the inside. They are served (on happy little sheep plates) with butter and raspberry jam, and a napkin is brought along with the scone. Everything here is of high quality, and that's one of the things that always comes to mind when I think of Gloagburn.

There is not usually any background music in Gloagburn (I'm not sure if there ever is, in fact), and because it's large and spacious and not too busy before and after the lunchtime rush, I've found it to be a great place to sit and write in the mornings.

When I think about which tearoom to visit on a particular occasion, my choice depends largely on what I want to get out of my experience there. First and foremost is usually the food and drink, but if I'm going on my own and want to work with my laptop or notebook, there are only a few tearooms I immediately think of as fitting the bill. Gloagburn is one of them. It's also an excellent place to go with company, and I've been here with a variety of friends and relatives.

The café is split into two sections, the inner section and the conservatory. There are sturdy wooden tables throughout, with wooden chairs inside and wickerwork chairs in the conservatory.

There are many attractions about this place, including plenty of free car parking outside the shop and café, and it's a great place to bring children. There is a duck pond, and there are various other animals that children are encouraged to introduce themselves to (they are fenced in) (the animals, not the children), such as sheep, goats and chickens.

There is also a little gravelled area with several plastic tractors that I have often observed children riding on.

Due to the space around the tearoom, there is also the fairly unique option of arriving here by helicopter. You would have to have your own helicopter, but I have seen one land in the grounds, and the occupants casually stroll into the café, sit down to coffee and a chat, and then toddle back to their chopper to take to the skies again.

The very interesting and well stocked farm shop attached to the café sells a selection of local and speciality foods, including the farm's own free range eggs, vegetables and preserves, and a range of gifts and kitchenware.

Gloagburn – useful information

Contact Gloagburn, Tibbermore, Perth, PH1 1QL
Tel: 01738 840864
www.gloagburnfarmshop.co.uk

Location 6 miles from the centre of Perth near the
hamlet of Tibbermore, signposted from the
A9, Stirling to Perth road, and from the A85,
Perth to Crieff road

Open every day all year (except 25 & 26 December;
1 & 2 January) 9.00am – 5.30pm

Access shop and café both wheelchair accessible,
with roomy accessible toilets

Children high chairs available

Payment credit cards accepted

Parking plenty free parking in the shop's own large car
park, including a number of disabled spaces

Size large

Alcohol café licensed

Library Café

"You can never get a cup of tea large enough or a book long enough to suit me." So said the author C S Lewis, and the Library Café has taken these words, along with other comments about tea and coffee from a number of famous writers, and decorated the walls of the café with them. This literary connection is very apt, since the café itself is housed within the A K Bell Library, Perth's central public lending library. Being a café in a library, it's not unusual to see customers sitting here perusing borrowed books and soaking up the bookish atmosphere of the place.

For me, the Library Café has often been the perfect place to sit and write, and indeed some of this book was written there, over many cups of golden tea and delicious fruit bran scones. Their scones are, I believe, supplied daily by Perth's Tower Bakery, and are always excellent, and the Fairtrade tea and coffee provides a consistently high quality brew.

In one corner of the café there are a few shelves of ex-library books for sale (at very cheap prices), which is a nice addition to the surroundings. There are also greetings cards and a few postcards for sale, and the café even sells stamps, so if you're on your holidays in Perth this could be the perfect opportunity to visit a nice tearoom and dash off a quick card or two while you're at it.

The chairs are mostly chrome-framed with wooden arms, lightly padded seats and padded backs, but there are a number of easy chairs and a couple of sofas at coffee tables, too. The café is popular with a range of people, including mums with babies and small children, and the spacious layout of the tables means that it's an easy place to wheel buggies and prams around. Perhaps partly due to the wide range and types of customer, there is a very relaxed and accepting atmosphere here. I've

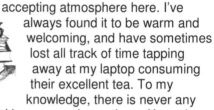

always found it to be warm and welcoming, and have sometimes lost all track of time tapping away at my laptop consuming their excellent tea. To my knowledge, there is never any music playing and in my experience the café can be a considerably quieter place to work in than the library itself.

There is a good choice of hot and cold food available all day. In the winter, hot food includes dishes such as macaroni cheese and chilli con carne, as well as soup, paninis, bacon rolls, baked potatoes and toasties, and there is a good selection of tray bakes and scones as well as a sponge cake or two.

Napkins, milk and cutlery are available from a counter at one end of the café, from which you help yourself. I like this feature, because it means you're not restricted to one napkin (which can be troublesome if you happen to spill your tea and need to mop it up), and if you need more milk you can go and refill your jug from a large jug on the counter without having to attract the attention of a waitress. On the subject of waitresses, this café does not have table service. When you come into the café you collect a tray (there are two sizes available, the standard size and a dinky wee one) and take what you would like from the chiller cabinet/cake counter, or order what you want in the way of hot food or beverages, on the way to the till.

In addition to standard tea and coffee, there are several herbal tea options, and as well as cakes and sandwiches there are small snacky things such as packets of crisps and some wrapped biscuits, e.g. Tunnock's Tea Cakes, Club biscuits and Kit-Kats. Without sacrificing quality, this must surely be one of the cheapest cafés in Perth.

Library Café – useful information

Contact York Place, Perth, PH2 8EP
Tel: 01738 477017
www.pkc.gov.uk (search for 'AK Bell library
café)

Location inside the AK Bell Library on York Place,
near the centre of Perth

Open Monday to Friday 9:30am – 4.30pm
Saturday 9:30am – 3.30pm

Access wheelchair accessible, with accessible toilets

Children high chairs available

Payment credit cards accepted

Parking two pay car parks at the library, plus on-
street parking meters nearby, slightly
cheaper parking available at the Station
Hotel car park a few minutes' walk away

Size large

Alcohol café not licensed

Giraffe Café

The Giraffe Café burgeons forth from the centre of Perth, with pots of flowers and plants beautifully displayed outside, brightening up the street and cheering shoppers on their way. Inside, it is a lovely, friendly cafe run by volunteers as a social enterprise on a not for profit basis.

The company that runs it (Giraffe Trading CIC) has set it up to enable disadvantaged adults who would otherwise struggle to find a role into the workplace, to gain employment and learn how to operate in a job. These employees are trained up using a 'buddy' system, buddies being appropriately trained volunteers who are there to provide support and encouragement to their trainees. I think that this thoughtful and kindly approach to things is partly what makes visiting the Giraffe Café such a friendly and positive experience.

Having been lured inside by the wonderful flowers outside, you find yourself in a tearoom that has been decorated and furnished in neutral shades. This provides a perfect backdrop for the framed pictures on the walls and the many colourful gifts on sale around the room. There are lots of items to browse amongst, including designer jewellery, mugs, cards, toiletries and Fair Isle knitwear. If you're lucky, you'll also spy a pile of cherry-filled luxury fruit scones on the counter.

I tend to think of this café as a tea/coffee and cakes sort of place, but they do also offer soups and toasties, and are currently in the process of securing premises next-door as a food preparation area, which will enable them to increase their menu to include some other as yet undeclared delights.

Amongst the cake options, which include sponge cake, biscuits, scones and traybakes, there are gluten-free options. In my experience, the tea and coffee are both very good and I particularly like the plain white, stylish, china. I find the teacups lovely to drink out of and some of the jugs are a most unusual and pleasing shape. They have a loyalty card that entitles you to a free hot drink when you've bought 9.

The Giraffe Café attracts regular customers, many of whom like to support the cause, but also appreciate the welcoming atmosphere and the luxury fruit scones. With its central location, it has to compete with the big coffee chains, but it does this brilliantly, providing something far more intimate and homely. Every time I see it from the outside with the flowers and plants arranged on the pavement, I feel chuffed that a volunteer-run café and shop has such a professional looking exterior. A lot of effort has obviously gone into making it look attractive. and eye-catching, and I think the hard work that has gone into it will, quite rightly, pay dividends.

Giraffe Café – useful information

Contact   51-53 South Street, Perth, PH2 8PD
Tel: 01738 449227
www.giraffe-trading.co.uk

Location   on South Street, towards the River Tay end

Open   Monday to Saturday 9:00am – 5:00pm
(also open on Sundays near Christmas
11:00am – 4:00pm)

Access   shop and cafe wheelchair accessible, no
accessible toilet, but publicly available
accessible toilets at nearby Ropemakers
Close and South Inch

Children   high chair available

Payment   credit cards accepted

Parking   on-street metered parking for short duration
on South Street including quite a number of
disabled spaces, metered parking on George
Street and Princes Street, large pay car parks
in Canal Street and South Inch

Size   medium

Alcohol   café not licensed

Macmillan coffee shop

This marvellous coffee shop has been run by volunteers since it opened in 1991. All funds raised go to the local Macmillan Support Group who help cancer patients in Perth and Kinross. For that reason alone it would seem a good idea to frequent it, but even without the charity aspect it is a very fine tearoom indeed. The only thing wrong with it is that it's not open all the time (it closes between the end of September and the beginning of April) but then that makes the time when it is open all the more special. Every year I wait impatiently for the day to come when it opens its doors again to the public and I can rush in and fill myself up with tasty goodies served by extremely delightful staff.

The year I wrote this book, 2012, my mum, my sister and I were amongst the first 12 customers to cross the threshold when the coffee shop re-opened for business in April, and as a thank you for our custom we were given our drinks for free! This would be generous anywhere, but at a tearoom that serves such good tea and coffee, it was a real bonus. Even when you're charged for all your purchases, you'll find that your purse isn't badly damaged by the experience, for the prices here are very good.

There are lots of wonderful home-baked delights to tempt the hungry visitor, including some of Perthshire's finest scones. Every day there are several types of scone available, e.g. plain, fruit, date and cinnamon, but whichever flavour you choose, your scone is guaranteed to be freshly baked and pretty close to scone perfection. There are plenty of other sweet options to choose from too, including sponge cakes, traybakes, pancakes and biscuits.

If you fancy something a bit more substantial there are delicious home-made soups, and sandwiches on offer with various fillings, all made to order and presented with a little salad garnish. Over the lunchtime period you can sometimes obtain a toastie or other hot treat, and there is always freshly brewed coffee on the go in a filter jug, from which you are welcome to a free top-up. The tea is very good and,* in addition to ordinary black tea, several herbal options are available.

One of the many things I love about this tearoom is the layout of crockery on the tables. Places are set (on pretty, wipe-clean, tablecloths) with a teacup and saucer, and a side plate and knife. A stack of napkins, all ready and waiting for your arrival, is available from

a little wooden holder with an animal on it (I like the cow). Whenever I visit I feel as if they've been expecting me to call and are well aware that I'll be needing a little something when I sit down.

Until recently I had thought that I must be one of this tearoom's biggest fans, but then I met someone who visits just about every day (sometimes twice on the same day), and realised I was actually a bit of a lightweight. I'm quite sure there are plenty of other people who feel very loyal to this place, because it really is an excellent institution.

When you enter the café, you come in through a small gift shop, which sells cards, jewellery, preserves, ornaments, bags and quite a few other things besides. One of the most exciting things sold in the gift shop, to my mind, is the Macmillan Coffee Shop's own recipe book. Here you will find recipes for many of the delicious foods available in the tearoom, and I can vouch for it being a very good buy. I've made quite a number of the recipes, with surprising success, and am looking forward to working my way through more of them. As with the café, all profits from the shop go to help cancer patients in the area, so it's well worth buying a little souvenir of your visit when you pop in. There's a visitors' book too, so you can leave an encouraging message for the enthusiastic staff who keep this splendid place operational.

Outside the building there are some seats for *al fresco* dining, and there is usually a rack of second-hand books for sale. Beyond the building there are woodland walks in the Quarrymill Woodland Park, run by The Gannochy Trust, who give Macmillan free use of the café's premises.

Macmillan Coffee Shop – useful information

Contact   Quarrymill Woodland Park, Isla Road, Perth,
               PH2 7HQ
               Tel: 01738 633890
               www.macmillancoffeeshop.webs.com

Location   on the A93 at the entrance to the woodland
               park, on the northern outskirts of Perth

Open   Monday to Saturday 10:00am – 4:30pm
               Open from early April to late September
               (actual dates vary every year)

Access   wheelchair accessible, with three accessible
               toilets

Children   high chairs available

Payment   credit cards not accepted

Parking   free car park at the front of the coffee shop,
               extra parking at Upper Springland, located
               opposite the entrance to Quarrymill

Size   medium

Alcohol   café not licensed

East Redstone Antiques

This is one of two antiques shops with cafés attached that I've included in this book, and I think it's a winning combination. Certain parts of Perthshire and Angus seem to be chock-full of rural antiques shops, not all of which have cafés, but the ones I like best are those where they've married these two delights under one roof. Whether or not you want to actually buy any antiques, just being surrounded by them creates an interesting atmosphere in which to take tea, have lunch or indulge in a tasty snack.

East Redstone is a beautifully kitted out tearoom, with lovely duck-patterned tablecloths and little bells on each table that you can ring for service. It's just off quite a fast road, but once you're inside you feel transported to a haven of elegance and calm.

In addition to soaking up the atmosphere, I like to come here for the very tasty Yorkshire tea (the coffee is also good) and the wonderful cakes. I've had a very lemony lemon drizzle cake here on more than one occasion, with lemon curd in the middle and crusty sugar on top, which was a little piece of citrusy cake heaven. East Redstone has also provided me with the most walnuty walnut cake I've ever tasted, packed with walnuts throughout the cake. That was the first cake I ever had here, and it sealed my fate; this was bound to become a favourite tearoom in the area.

The menu is written up on a board at one end of the tearoom, and includes tasty home-made soup, sandwiches and omelettes, to complement the sweet treats. There is a soup and sandwich deal too, and if you're having lunch here with a chum, I recommend getting the soup and sharing a sandwich. This will, hopefully, leave you with room for a delicious cake, and some of their excellent tea or coffee to wash it down with.

The seating is mostly dining chairs at tables, but there is also a sofa and armchair with a coffee table, next to which is a pile of magazines that you can leaf through at your leisure. Instrumental music is usually playing in the background, and I've noticed that the friendly staff are good at making their customers feel welcome.

Before or after your refreshments you will almost certainly want to have a little wander round the shop. The main part of this is attached to the tearoom, indeed you have to walk through it to get to the tearoom, and there's a separate section across the courtyard. Every time I visit there are new and interesting items for sale, from furniture to china, glassware, silver and books. There are also a few new bits and bobs for sale, such as soaps, candles, cards and jewellery.

East Redstone Antique – useful information

Contact   East Redstone Farm, Burrelton, Blairgowrie,
                 Perthshire, PH13 9PR
                 Telephone: 01821 650 555
                 www.antiques-atlas.com/antiqueseastredstone

Location   just off the A94 about 4 miles south-west of
                 Coupar Angus and 6 miles north-east of
                 Scone

Open   Tuesday to Saturday 10:30am – 4.00pm
                 (closed Sunday and Monday), reduced hours
                 in winter, please phone for details

Access   wheelchair accessible, with accessible toilet

Children   high chairs not available

Payment   credit cards accepted

Parking   free car park in the gravelled courtyard
                 outside

Size   medium

Alcohol   café not licensed

Culdees

Culdees Tearoom is housed in what must be quite an old whitewashed building down a little lane in the charming village of Abernethy. From the outside I think it looks very promising, and it lives up to its billing inside.

When you step through the door you find yourself in a lovely old-fashioned room, with painted stone walls, an old fireplace and an interesting coloured glass panel in the ceiling. It's the sort of room in which I feel, on sitting down at a table, I should be removing a pair of good quality leather gloves and placing them neatly on top of my matching handbag, while respectfully keeping my hat on.

There is a wonderful selection of cakes and teas, as well as Italian style coffees. The cakes include such delights as lemon drizzle cake, chocolate cake, pistachio coffee cake and Victoria sponge. There are also some traybakes, pancakes, fruit loaf and delicious freshly baked scones. Teas available include Earl Grey, Lady Grey, Lapsang Souchong and a number of herbal varieties, as well as standard black tea.

The savoury food menu is impressively varied for a small place like this, ranging from bacon, egg and chips to rice dishes (including a vegetarian option), salads, jacket potatoes, sandwiches and baguettes. A pepper grinder and bottle of salad dressing are available on the table so that you can help yourself, if required (both of these details always get a thumbs-up from me).

In addition to being a tearoom, Culdees is a picture  framing shop and one wall of the room is dedicated to a selection of frame samples. On at least two occasions when I've been in for some refreshment there have been people getting pictures framed, so this is obviously a good little business. I have some pictures myself that need framing and I keep meaning to take them to Culdees. The idea of combining this little task with taking tea and perhaps one of their excellent scones is very appealing.

Next-door to Culdees is a most interesting building, the historic round tower, to which Culdees holds the key (you can borrow it and slog up to the top of the tower for fine views if you feel up to it – worth it when you know you can get a nice cup of tea and a tasty treat at the bottom). The tearoom is named after the Culdee monks who built the tower, apparently around 1100AD. If this interests you, you may also like to visit the museum just down the road. Please see the museum's website for opening times (May-October): www.museumofabernethy.co.uk

Culdees – useful information

Contact   School Wynd, Abernethy, Perthshire, PH2 9JJ
Tel: 01738 850455

Location   near the centre of Abernethy village, next to the round tower and near the museum

Open   Tuesday to Saturday 10.00am – 5.00pm (closed Sunday and Monday)

Access   two steps up to the café entrance from the street, toilets not wheelchair accessible

Children   high chairs available

Payment   credit cards not accepted

Parking   free on-street parking in Abernethy close to the tearoom

Size   medium

Alcohol   café not licensed

The Tufted Duck Tearoom is a delightful little snackery situated in the longest established antiques centre in Perthshire. The antiques centre comprises a collection of lovely Georgian farm buildings that form a sort of tiny hamlet of antique shops in the small village of Rait, not far from Perth.

I've had excellent service from the staff in every tearoom mentioned in this book, but if I were giving out a prize for the most polite and gentlemanly service experienced anywhere, it would have to go to The Tufted Duck. On every occasion I have visited this tearoom, from the very first time to the most recent visit, I have been greeted warmly and with great courtesy by the chap who runs it. I'm slightly nervous about making great claims regarding service because, as mentioned in Le Jardin Café's review, any normal human being has an off day every now and then, but as with Le Jardin Café, I feel quite confident that these are very few and far between at The Tufted Duck.

The menu is quite small, as befits a small tearoom, but it does include soup and toasted rolls, as well as cold rolls, sandwiches, cakes and scones. Bakery items, often including a variety of rolls, are supplied fresh daily by Fisher and Donaldson of Cupar, and I can vouch for the oatie rolls being very good. Local produce, such as free range eggs and home-cured meats, are used where available. Sandwiches and rolls are made up to order, and although they don't come with a side salad or any other accoutrements, the quality is very good. The sweet treats vary from day to day and include options such as carrot cake, shortbread, muffins and delicious individual little fruit pies. Food can be taken away for picnics, and there are picnic tables outside. The tea (several varieties available) and coffee are very good, and the coffee is Italian style.

One of the things I like to find in a tearoom is a pepper grinder on the table, rather than the sort of powdery pepper you shake out of a cellar, and The Tufted Duck has salt and pepper grinders on every table. There are lovely black and white floor tiles on the tearoom floor, which make me think of John Tenniel's illustrations in *Alice through the looking glass*, which is very fitting for somewhere that has a sort of magical storybook feel to it.

There are newspapers available in the tearoom, and no lack of things to look at in the antique shop. As well as the various antiques for sale in the shop, there are some locally crafted products such as scarves and cards. There are some fine lampposts to be seen in the nearby village of Rait, if you care to take a stroll along the road.

The Tufted Duck Tearoom – useful information

Contact
The Cart Shed, Rait Antique Centre, Rait, Perthshire, PH2 7RT
Tel: 01821 670760
www.timhardie.com/THE-TUFTED-DUCK-COFFEE-SHOP

Location
next to the small village of Rait, about 1 mile west of the A90 roughly midway between Dundee and Perth (slightly closer to Perth), Rait Antiques Centre signposted from the A90

Open
Monday to Saturday 10:00am – 5:00pm
Sunday 12:00am – 5:00pm

Access
wheelchair accessible, accessible toilets in another building of the antiques centre

Children
high chairs available

Payment
credit and debit cards accepted

Parking
plenty of free car parking in the gravelled area outside The Tufted Duck and throughout the antiques centre

Size
medium

Alcohol
café not licensed

T Ann Cake

T Ann Cake is a surprising café and bakehouse tucked away down a side street near the city centre in Dundee. Something about it reminds me of my student days in Edinburgh. It's lovably quirky, with tree branches and bunting suspended from the ceiling, mismatched vintage china, and paintings of coats and handbags beneath the coat-hooks on the wall.

Virtually all the food in the café is made on the premises by the busy bakehouse staff who start early in the morning and, if cakes run out during the day, bake fresh cakes in the afternoon, too. They have several tempting and delicious sponge cakes every day, as well as muffins, scones and a few traybakes. Their sponge cakes are really excellent and I have great difficulty in choosing between them. Their lime and coconut cake is one of my favourites, beautifully decorated with toasted coconut and shavings of lime peel and with really excellent icing. I'm not much of an icing fan on the whole, but I wolf up the icing at T Ann Cake with great relish.

The menu, which is chalked up on a blackboard near the counter, changes frequently, and in terms of savouries they have a very interesting selection of options, e.g. sweet potato, ginger, lentil and star anise soup (served with their own granary bread) and roasted red pepper and chick pea dip served with flat bread. Some of the choices are suitable for vegetarians, vegans and those who need their food to be gluten-free. They also offer tasty breakfasts, which include their own granola with milk or yoghurt and honey, and home-made coconut bread.

The tea and coffee are both very good, the coffee being Fairtrade, organic and quite strong, and the tea being Teapigs or Twinings selections. The teapots come with knitted tea cosies on them (one of them has a knitted pig on top), and tea is served in delicate china teacups.

Most of the seating is made up of dining tables and chairs, but there are some arm chairs and a sofa towards the front of the café. You can watch what's going on in the kitchen while you wait for your food, because it's all open plan, with the kitchen at the back of the room. I particularly enjoyed watching one of the staff picking out lettuce leaves for my salad one day, inspecting each one carefully to see that it was up to the job. I have frequently found woebegone lettuce in salads but I think this highly unlikely at T Ann Cake.

If you like a bit of funky music, you will perhaps enjoy what they play in here. I haven't actually ever seen customers up on the floor boogying to the sounds, but I imagine it must happen sometimes. The music is very much a part of the whole atmosphere of the place, being (in my experience) a mixture of blues, soul and funk, with the odd bit of Gershwin thrown in.

T Ann Cake – useful information

Contact   27 Exchange Street, Dundee, DD1 3DJ
Tel: 01382 203950
www.t-ann-cake.blogspot.co.uk

Location   towards the south-east of the city centre, a
few minutes' walk from the High Street down
towards the docks

Open   Tuesday to Friday 10:00am – 5:00pm
Saturday 10:00am – 4:00pm
(closed Sunday and Monday)

Access   wheelchair accessible, with accessible toilet
(although quite a tight fit)

Children   high chairs available

Payment   credit cards accepted

Parking   metered on-street parking in Exchange Street
and other nearby streets for up to 1 hour,
longer stay parking in nearby Shore Terrace
car park

Size   medium

Alcohol   café not licensed

Parrot Café

The overwhelming impression I had on first visiting The Parrot Café was that I had stepped back into the 1950s. I could almost imagine Miss Marple coming in with her little handbag and hat and politely ordering a pot of tea and a scone. This café is, I feel, a place where jangled nerves could be calmed and a detective's brain could come up with a solution to the most complex of murder mysteries. There is a wonderful air of tranquillity and peace about it, and I think it would be an excellent place to come before an interview or other nerve-wracking event.

Only a pavement and a door separate it from the city outside, and yet it's incredibly quiet inside. I daresay one could be left with quite a different impression if visiting when screaming children were present, but it seems to attract an older, very well behaved, clientele. On my first visit it was so quiet that, despite there being 5 other diners present, I could easily hear the gentle ticking of a wooden-cased clock hanging on a wall on the opposite side of the room. On another occasion the soft murmur of Radio 4 was coming from the kitchens.

The woodwork of the tables, chairs and other bits of furniture is all of the same type and colour, and ties in with the parquet flooring. This repetition of wood around the room enhances the feeling of uniform calm.

In some ways it's quite spartan, with clean, plain surfaces and little decoration, apart from some quite brightly coloured canvases around the walls, produced from photographs taken by an elderly gentleman who sells them here. There are one or two parrots hanging discreetly, but there is a general lack of fussiness about the décor. The lighting is very pleasant, a combination of natural daylight and halogen spotlights.

Menus are brought if desired, and there are daily specials written up on a blackboard, which tend to be larger meals than those contained in the menu. As an example, the last time I was there the specials included butternut, sage and mascarpone risotto, and fish and chips. There is also a daily dessert on offer, e.g. rhubarb bread pudding.

Aside from the specials, hot food includes grilled cheese on toast (with various added options, such as onion or ham) and baked potatoes. There are also sandwiches, served on home-made rye bread, scones, a traybake or two and several moist-looking tea breads, e.g. tea brack, gingerbread, walnut and sultana loaf (all available for viewing under hygienically clingfilm-wrapped plates on a wooden counter). In my experience, it is worth coming here for the jam alone. If you order a scone and add the home-made raspberry jam to your order, you are in for a real treat. I'm not always much of a one for jam on scones, but I delight in ladling this stuff on with gusto, it's so delicious (you can sometimes buy some to take home). Although the scones would be fine without jam, they're not particularly sweet and they become something really special when all jammed up. A well-pouring teapot of the excellent leaf tea contains enough for two cupfuls, and two cupfuls of coffee can be obtained from one of their small cafétieres (a large size is also available).

I can't absolutely guarantee this, and it may be that you are generally a very calm person, but I would be surprised if you didn't leave this café feeling considerably calmer than when you went in. It's hard to describe an atmosphere but, to my mind at least, there is something almost ecclesiastical about this place. As far as I'm aware the building has no historical church connection, but it feels to me almost as if the Parrot Café had been some sort of monastic retreat in a previous life.

Parrot Cafe – useful information

Contact   Parrot Café, 91 Perth Road, Dundee,
DD1 4HZ
Tel: 01382 206277

Location   on the west side of the city, near the
University

Open   Tuesday to Friday 10.00am – 5.00pm,
Saturday 10.00am – 4.00pm (closed Sunday
and Monday)

Access   wheelchair accessible, with accessible toilet

Children   one clip-on baby chair available

Payment   credit cards not accepted (small surcharge for
cheques under £10.00)

Parking   2 on-street spaces right outside the café, in
which you can park for free for up to 45
minutes, several pay car parks nearby, but
can be extremely busy

Size   medium

Alcohol   café not licensed

Le Jardin Café

Of all the tearooms in this book, Le Jardin Café is probably the one I've been visiting for longest. Its situation, just off the M90 between Edinburgh and Perth, has made it a very convenient stopping off place when travelling between the two cities, and, to my knowledge, there is nothing to equal it in the area. I have occasionally popped into the service station nearby for a quick loo stop, but if I want something to eat and drink during Le Jardin Café's opening hours, there's no competition.

The café is inside Dobbies garden centre, and I often enjoy a little wander round the gifts and plants before or after my refreshments in the tearoom.

It's a very popular place with locals and travellers alike, and although I have sometimes had to wait a few minutes for a table, the service is quick, efficient and friendly. Even when the whole place looks as if it's going like a fair, the staff seem to keep on top of it all with admirable calm and competence.

There is a vibrancy and liveliness about this tearoom, and perhaps this is due to it being a family run business that has been on the go – with many of the same staff – for years, and they've got things down to a fine art. I hate to tempt fate by saying this, and of course everyone has an off day once in a while, but I am constantly impressed by the way Le Jardin Café is run, from the training of the staff to the delivery of consistently good food.

The menu includes a number of excellent hot choices, such as baked potatoes, pasta dishes, soup and toasties (I particularly like the spinach and ricotta cannelloni). There are also various sandwiches and salads, and many of the main dishes include an unusually varied side salad. I think the salads, whether as main meals or extras on the side, are particularly good, being very fresh and including interesting touches, such as very thin slices of apple. I think one of the reasons I'm so fond of the cannelloni dish is that it comes with a lovely salad and a crusty roll, all of which combines to make my idea of a perfect lunch.

The café is split into two areas, the main indoor area and a conservatory. I find both very pleasant places to sit, and there is a cosy feel to both rooms, despite the tiled floor and other hard surfaces.

In one corner of the main room there is a glass-fronted cabinet full of cakes, scones, traybakes and other tempting treats, such as big cream meringues and strawberry tarts. There is also a selection of interesting ice creams that you can have one or more scoops of in a bowl, including a very sweet Scottish tablet ice cream, to which I am quite partial (the mint one is also excellent – very minty!).

Le Jardin Café – useful information

Contact   Le Jardin Café, Turfhills, Kinross,
KY13 0NQ
Tel: 01577 863 308

Location   just off the M90 at junction 6, within
Dobbies garden centre next to the Moto
service station and BP garage

Open   every day 9:30am – 5:00pm

Access   wheelchair accessible, with accessible
toilet

Children   high chairs available

Payment   credit cards accepted

Parking   plenty of free parking in Dobbies car park
right outside the café

Size   large

Alcohol   café licensed

Area Index

Map Index